31016000015632

18556

DATE DUE

			PRINTED IN U.S.A.

NASA

Published by Smart Apple Media

123 South Broad Street

Mankato, Minnesota 56001

Photos: nasa/kennedy space center; page 19—nasa/jpl/caltech

Design and Production: EvansDay Design

Library of Congress Cataloging-in-Publication Data

Hakkila, Jon Eric, 1957–

NASA / by Jon Hakkila and Adele D. Richardson

p. cm. — (Above and beyond)

Includes index.

Summary: Examines the functions of NASA and the impact of

its various space exploration programs.

ISBN 1-58340-050-8

1. United States—National Aeronautics and Space Administra-

tion—Juvenile literature. 2. Outer space—Exploration—United

States—Juvenile literature. 3. Astronautics—United States—

Juvenile literature. [1. United States. 2. National Aeronautics

and Space Administration.] I. Richardson, Adele, 1966–. II. Title.

III. Series: Above and beyond (Mankato, Minn.)

TL521.312.H32   1999

629.4'0973—DC21   98-20888

First edition

1 3 5 7 9 8 6 4 2

18556

NASA

DR. JON HAKKILA & ADELE D. RICHARDSON

ABOVE & BEYOND

THE MISSION CONTROL CENTER in Houston, Texas, buzzed with activity on June 2, 1998 ✳ As people scurried about, flight controllers sat at computer consoles, talking into their headset microphones ✳ Suddenly, the hum of voices was drowned out by a booming loudspeaker: "three . . . two . . . one . . . and liftoff!" ✳ The space shuttle *Discovery* was on its way to its ninth and final *Mir* docking mission ✳ National Aeronautics and Space Administration (NASA) technicians cheered as the shuttle rose into the sky, but their job was just beginning ✳ For the next 10 days, they would monitor the shuttle's voyage around the clock ✳

America's Space Program

In 1957, the **space race** began when the Soviet Union surprised the world by launching *Sputnik 1*, the first man-made **satellite**. *Sputnik 1*'s successful launch frightened many Americans, who feared that the Soviets might use their technology to launch missiles at the United States. Government offices were flooded with telephone calls and letters as the public demanded the immediate launching of American satellites.

Facing this public outcry, the U.S. Congress encouraged President Dwight D. Eisenhower to establish America's presence in space. At that time, the National Advisory Committee of **Aeronautics** (NACA), as well as many other government agencies, including the Army, Navy, and Air Force military branches, were all working separately to develop satellites. In July 1958, the Space Act changed that. With the act's passing, the National Aeronautics and Space Administration was officially created on October 1, 1958. From then on, all space-related programs would be developed and managed through this one agency.

According to the Space Act, NASA's responsibilities are to conduct flight research both within and outside of

Earth's atmosphere; to develop, build, test, and operate space vehicles (both manned and unmanned); to explore space with both manned and unmanned vehicles; to work with other nations on projects for peaceful uses of space; and to make its findings available to the public.

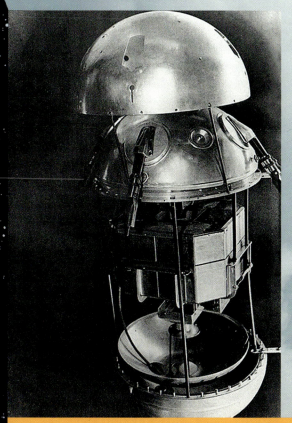

Sputnik 1 *(left)*, the first man-made satellite, is prepared for launch *(right)*.

The **space race**—between Americans and Russians—was a race for space supremacy.

A **satellite** is an object— natural or man-made—that orbits a celestial body.

Aeronautics is the science of flight or aircraft operation.

One of the first successes for NASA was the 1959 launching of *Pioneer 4*, the first space exploration vehicle to land on the moon. Later, in May 1961, astronaut Alan Shepard became the first American in space.

Today, NASA has offices all over the country. NASA Headquarters (HQ), located in Washington, D.C., is where all programs are planned, developed, and managed. NASA HQ prepares proposals, such as ideas for new programs or updates to existing ones, and presents them to the president and Congress. The president chooses the programs he feels should be developed, and Congress decides how much money the agency will receive to fund them. NASA HQ then takes the money and distributes it to the appropriate areas.

Ultimately, everything NASA does is for the benefit of the public. This is only appropriate, since it is the public's tax money that funds most of NASA's programs. Over the years, NASA has been divided into four **enterprises** to carry out the agency's responsibilities as outlined in the

Space Act. These enterprises are Mission to Planet Earth (MTPE), Space Science, Human Exploration and Development of Space (HEDS), and Aeronautics and Space Transportation Technology (ASTT). All of NASA's programs fall into one of these four enterprises; many times, two or more work together to achieve a common goal.

*NASA's **enterprises** are four program offices created to develop the activities of the agency.*

An astronaut walks on the moon, then returns to Earth via an ocean landing.

Earth and Beyond

In 1991, Mission to Planet Earth (MTPE) was created. This program uses **remote sensing satellites** to study all aspects of Earth's environment: air, water, land, and vegetation. *Landsat* and *Seasat* are two satellites that have helped NASA monitor land use and crop growth, as well as the movement of the oceans. Other satellites have measured the temperatures of rock formations, studied the earth's magnetic field, and watched for changes in the planet's surface during earthquakes and volcanic eruptions. Meteorologists also rely on weather satellites to help them predict the weather.

Some of the goals of MTPE are to increase our understanding of Earth's environment; to identify natural changes that occur on the planet—especially concerning an area's climate; to understand the effects of human activities on an environment; and to help predict what the consequences of any such effects may be.

NASA facilities, such as the Dryden Flight Research Center in California and the Goddard Space Flight Center in Maryland, make public all satellite findings so that people

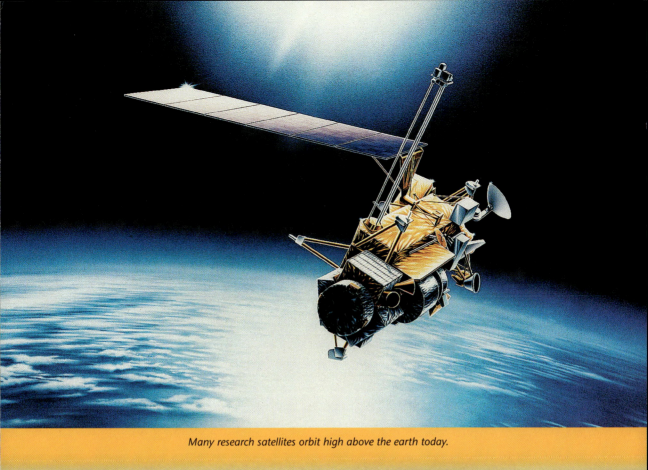

Many research satellites orbit high above the earth today.

are well-informed and can make the decisions necessary to keep their part of the world healthy.

By studying information about the past and the present, scientists can form an idea of what Earth's future may be like. If they are able to detect serious problems, such as a growing hole in the ozone layer, steps can be taken to make the necessary changes before irreversible damage is done.

The Space Science enterprise has been around since NASA

Remote sensing satellites *are spacecraft used to study the earth from space.*

was created. Through this program, many unmanned satellites have been launched to explore the wonders of our **solar system**. By studying planets other than our own, scientists hope to gain new knowledge of the universe—information that may offer clues to the earth's past and future.

Space Science is a huge enterprise, often using the resources of other enterprises and working in partnership with universities and private businesses. The missions of this program are to explore the solar system; to find and learn about distant planets around other suns; and to search for life beyond Earth.

To carry out these missions, Space Science is deeply involved in the research, development, and building of vehicles and equipment for space travel. Some of the more well-known space exploration vehicles that have been developed through Space Science are the *Voyager* spacecraft in the 1970s and the recent *Mars Pathfinder* explorers.

Space Science has great plans for the future of space exploration. **Observatories** are being planned and developed that will allow scientists to see farther into deep space, possibly unlocking some of the universe's greatest mysteries. This enterprise hopes to establish a constant

A **solar system** *is a star and the celestial bodies that orbit it.*

An **observatory** *is a structure from which outer space can be studied.*

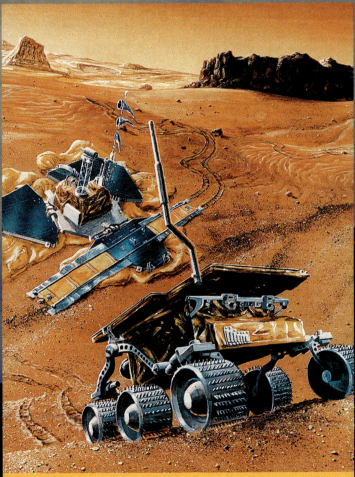

NASA technology has created the Voyager *spacecraft (top), and the* Mars Pathfinder *rover (bottom).*

presence in outer space, preparing for the day when humans will land on and explore other planets.

Aeronautics and Space Transportation Technology (ASTT) is another of NASA's enterprises. This branch deals not only with spacecraft development, but with the development of safe airplane systems here on Earth as well.

ASTT has several impressive goals concerning air transportation that it hopes to achieve before the year 2020. Research is currently being done that is leading to the construction of better aircraft. One of ASTT's goals is to produce airplanes that are 10 times safer for passengers than those of the late 1990s. NASA is working to make

NASA is constantly working on improvements to air travel, including new high-speed aircraft designs.

planes healthier for the environment as well by cutting down on the engine noise and chemicals that are discharged into the air. Astt also hopes that its discoveries will cut the price of air travel in half.

As Astt continues to work on better and safer aircraft, it will also help create faster airplanes. This will require a total change in the way aircraft are designed, constructed, and operated. Astt's goal is to reduce the time needed to travel overseas in half, for both cheaper and faster air transportation.

The program also has plans for future space vehicles. By designing and building improved reusable vehicles

The agency hopes to double the speed of current air transportation by the year 2020.

similar to the space shuttle, ASTT is working to reduce the cost of transporting materials into space. What costs consumers more than $10,000 a pound to place in orbit today would cost only $100 per pound by the year 2020. ASTT will continue to work closely with the other enterprises to develop research spacecraft for use in exploring our solar system.

NASA's fourth enterprise is Human Exploration and Development of Space (HEDS). This branch of NASA has four main goals that it works toward with the help of the other NASA enterprises and private businesses. These goals are to increase our knowledge of nature by studying the space environment; to explore the solar system and establish human presence where possible; to achieve low-cost, routine space travel; and to help make life on Earth better through the knowledge gained by people living and working in space.

HEDS researchers work in both the science and technology fields. These people work on scientific experiments conducted in space and have helped with the development of **robotics** for missions to other planets.

The two most likely places for future space colonies are

Robotics *is the branch of science dealing with the design, construction, and operation of robots.*

NASA has played a major role in constructing the International Space Station.

the moon and Mars. To learn more about prolonged living in space, HEDS works on missions closer to Earth, such as making improvements to the space shuttle and building the International Space Station.

Like all other NASA enterprises, HEDS has challenging goals. Only a lot of hard work and dedication from everyone involved will turn these ideas into reality. But even as the programs make new discoveries about space through daring and dangerous missions, the agency always puts the safety of Earth and its inhabitants first.

Centers Nationwide

All of NASA's research and programs are carried out through its nine centers and the Jet Propulsion Laboratory. These sites are located all over the continental U.S., and each serves a specific purpose.

Ames Research Center, located in Mountain View, California, is one of NASA's larger centers. Ames was originally founded on December 20, 1939, and became part of NASA when the agency was created in 1958. This center is responsible for **aerospace** research and technology; it is also a national center for computer research.

The Dryden Flight Research Center, located in Edwards, California, was established on September 20, 1946. Like Ames, this center later became part of NASA. Scientists at Dryden are devoted to the study of Earth's atmosphere and flight operations within the atmosphere.

Across the country—in Greenbelt, Maryland—is the Goddard Space Flight Center. This NASA site was created on May 1, 1959, and is another of NASA's larger centers. Goddard's missions focus on the scientific study of Earth, the solar system, and the universe.

The Jet Propulsion Laboratory of Pasadena, California, was established on November 1, 1944. This unique laboratory, managed by the California Institute of Technology, deals mainly with the robotic exploration of our solar system and deep space.

Houston, Texas, is the home of the Johnson Space Center. Since its founding in September 1961, this center has been the site for **astronaut** selection and training. Johnson is also responsible for the planning of all manned space flight missions. Once a rocket or shuttle leaves the launch pad of another NASA site, the Johnson Space Cen-

Whether in training or during a mission, astronaut safety is always NASA's top priority.

Aerospace is the study of Earth's atmosphere and the space beyond.

An **astronaut** is a person who travels above Earth's atmosphere.

ter takes complete control of the mission until the astronauts have landed back on Earth.

One of NASA's best-known centers is the Kennedy Space Center in Cape Canaveral, Florida. On October 1, 1949, Cape Canaveral was chosen by the U.S. government as the nation's missile launch site. Later, in November 1964, it was renamed the Kennedy Space Center in honor of the late president John F. Kennedy. All of today's space shuttles and other spacecraft are launched from this center; all manned rockets in the past also left Earth from this site.

The Langley Research Center in Hampton, Virginia, was originally established in 1917. Langley is involved with aircraft and spacecraft development, as well as the study of Earth's environment and atmosphere.

New technologies in space power and communications are developed at the Lewis Research Center. This center is located in Cleveland, Ohio, and is the only NASA center located in the midwestern United States. Lewis was founded on January 31, 1941.

A shuttle launch is always a thrilling event at the Kennedy Space Center.

The Marshall Space Flight Center in Huntsville, Alabama, is yet another of NASA's large centers. Established on July 1, 1960, Marshall is where the agency's rocket engines are developed. The site is mainly responsible for **microgravity research**, as well as many other experiments that are conducted on board space shuttles in orbit.

In Bay St. Louis, Mississippi, is a NASA center that was known as the Mississippi Test Facility during the 1960s. In June 1974, the name was changed to the National Space Technology Laboratories. Today, the site is known as the Stennis Space Center and is NASA's main center for rocket engine testing. Stennis is also deeply involved in studying changes in the earth through remote sensing satellites.

Microgravity research *are studies and experiments done in low-gravity environments.*

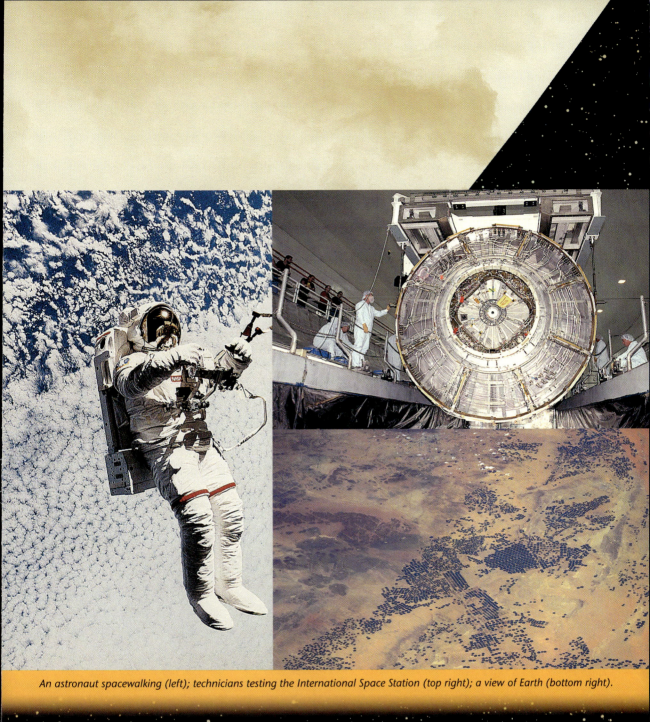

An astronaut spacewalking (left); technicians testing the International Space Station (top right); a view of Earth (bottom right).

Jobs at NASA

Working for NASA can be an exciting and rewarding experience. Today, the agency has nearly 18,000 employees, all working at Headquarters and in the NASA centers. The primary requirement to work for the agency is a good education.

More than half of NASA's work force is made up of scientists and engineers involved in the field of aerospace. Some of them study Earth and the universe, while others are involved in designing, building, and testing rockets and space vehicles. Also working for NASA are scientists who are well-educated in astronomy, chemistry, physics, and geology (for studying the surface of other planets). Also included in this group are biologists, medical doctors, and nurses.

The next largest group of NASA employees are the administrative professionals. These people specialize in certain areas that include dealing with the public, hiring employees, management, accounting, law, and hiring contractors to build rocket engines and parts. To be employed in this area of NASA, a person must have a college degree or a lot of special training for a particular job.

Still, there are many other important jobs in the NASA work force. Secretaries and assistants keep NASA's offices running smoothly; clerks are necessary for purchasing equipment and supplies, and assistants are needed to help scientists working in the laboratories.

Shuttle astronauts (top) and Hubble Space Telescope *technicians (bottom) are just a few of the many NASA employees.*

The two best-known jobs at NASA are probably those of the astronaut and the **flight director**. People who want to become astronauts must be in top physical and mental condition before they are even considered for the job. Once they have met all of NASA's requirements, they go through one year's worth of training at the Johnson Space Center. There they learn everything there is to know about shuttle construction, flight, and life in space. NASA employs two types of astronauts: **pilot astronauts** and **mission specialists**.

A third type of astronaut are the **payload specialists**. These astronauts usually work for the owner of the payload, or cargo, going into space. Even though they are not NASA employees, they must still go through astronaut training and have their mission approved by the agency.

The other most visible NASA job is that of the flight director. The job of the flight director begins as soon as a

A **flight director** *is the person in charge of Mission Control during a space flight.*

A **pilot astronaut** *is an astronaut who flies the shuttle.*

Mission specialists inspect a shuttle's cargo bay (left); pilot astronauts need a lot of flight experience (right).

shuttle leaves the launch pad and continues until it rolls to a stop back on Earth. The flight director is in charge of Mission Control during space flight and is responsible for all decisions made regarding the spacecraft during that time.

When employees in high positions retire or leave NASA, the agency prefers to promote people from within NASA. When a lower position opens up that must be filled, a qualified person straight from college is usually hired. NASA hires only the best, which usually means those with the most thorough education.

A **mission specialist** *is an astronaut trained to conduct scientific experiments.*

A **payload specialist** *is an astronaut who handles the cargo on a specific mission.*

27

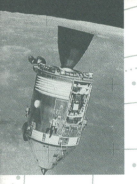

The Future

The future of NASA should prove to be just as exciting as its past. One vehicle, called *Stardust*, is scheduled for launch in 1999. The goal of its mission is to collect material from a comet and bring it back to Earth for study. NASA also plans to launch more orbital telescopes that will allow scientists to glimpse even farther into the universe.

The success of the Mars Pathfinder Mission, which landed exploratory equipment on Mars, has led to a full schedule of future trips to the "red planet." These missions include Surveyor 98, a two-part mission that will study both the atmosphere and the landscape of Mars. More trips are planned in 2001 and 2003. The *Mars Sample Return* spacecraft is scheduled for launch in 2005. If successful, it will collect samples from the landscape and return them to Earth for further study in the year 2008.

Our own planet will not be left out of NASA's future plans either. Several remote sensing satellites are being prepared for launch, and satellites that will map the ozone layer and monitor the amount of global rainfall are just a few of the other upcoming missions.

The Pathfinder *lander and rover exploring the surface of Mars.*

Perhaps NASA's best-known future mission is the International Space Station, a project NASA hopes to have built by January 2004. The station is part of a cooperative program between the U.S. and 15 other countries: Belgium, Brazil, Canada, Denmark, France, Germany, Italy, Japan, the Netherlands, Norway, Russia, Spain, Sweden, Switzerland, and the United Kingdom. It will be assembled in space from pieces carried up by space shuttles and will orbit about 220 miles (354 km) above Earth.

The goal of the Space Station program is to create a permanent orbiting science laboratory where medical experiments can be conducted in a gravity-free environment. Medical drugs and diseases often react differently in space, so scientists hope to be able to examine and treat illnesses differently than they do on Earth.

Manned flight to unexplored realms of space may begin once again in the near future. Many people have imagined a permanent base on the moon and have dreamt of trips to Mars. Although these goals may seem distant now, so did the idea of landing a man on the moon when NASA was founded in 1958. For more than 40 years, NASA has played an enormous role in some of civilization's most important accomplishments, and it will continue to do so in the new millennium.

NASA's growing space station technology will pave the way to future exploration milestones.

INDEX